DANCING WITH DOGS

A step-by-step guide to Freestyle

Richard Curtis

ABOUT THE AUTHOR

Richard Curtis has been training dogs since 1982 and was involved in Competitive Obedience before taking up Heelwork To Music.

He created his first routines at home and has had considerable success in competitions. He is also a judge and runs his own training courses.

As an Obedience instructor, Richard is aware of the difficulties of training different breeds, so his methods have been devised and tested with dogs of all sizes.

ACKNOWLEDGEMENTS

Many thanks to the following who appear in the book: Barbara Whitmarsh and Jesse the Golden Retriever; Renée Patience and Koko the Boxer; Lynda Levett, Ben the Maltese and Zoey the GSD; and to my own dogs – Border Collies Jazz and Sybil, and Disco, a Portuguese Water Dog. Thanks also to Carolyn Scott and Rookie the Golden Retriever (pictures on pages one and eight).

Published by Ringpress Books

A Division of INTERPET Publishing

Vincent Lane, Dorking, Surrey RH4 3YX

Designed by Rob Benson

ISBN 1 86054 267 0

Printed and bound in Hong Kong through Printworks International

0 9 8 7 6 5 4 3 2 1

Contents

1 How It All Started

In the UK, Heelwork To Music was the inspiration of two people: John Gilbert and Mary Ray. Mary Ray, a top Obedience and Agility handler and trainer, had always been noted for her superb deportment and smooth, effortless heelwork with her dogs. In 1990, John Gilbert, another Obedience and Agility trainer and handler, asked Mary to put together a heelwork routine to certain pieces of music, as part of an evening demonstration. From this start, Mary was asked to repeat this performance in 1992, and then did a demonstration at Crufts.

People were captivated by the new discipline – even though, at this early stage, it was no more than pure competition-style heelwork put to music. Mary continued her demonstrations at various events, and the next handler to start to show a significant interest in the sport was Donelda Guy from the Channel Islands.

In 1995, Donelda put together a demonstration with her own dog. Since then, Donelda has become a driving force behind Heelwork To Music in the UK; her flamboyant and innovative style has attracted many admirers. Donelda started to use a variety of moves in her routines, going beyond heelwork and working with her dog at a distance, which was the start of a more Freestyle approach to the discipline.

The first competition was masterminded by top Agility trainer Peter Lewis, in association with Rugby Dog Training Club. It was first held in 1996 at Coventry, and has become the main Heelwork To Music event of the year. At this stage, classes were limited, and few rules had been devised. For the first three years of the competition, Mary Ray did not compete, giving others the opportunity to catch up with her skills.

Meanwhile, Mary's Heelwork To Music demonstration was a regular feature at Crufts, and her routines, such as *Riverdance*, and, more recently, *The Sorcerer's Apprentice*, attracted lots of media attention. As a result, Mary was invited overseas to Switzerland, Denmark, Austria and South Africa to promote the sport, and to show how people can get started.

TRANSATLANTIC LINKS

While Heelwork To Music was developing in the UK, there was a parallel development in Canada and the USA. In 1992, Terry Arnold got involved in the new discipline, and now a number of organisations hold competitions throughout the States. Sandra Davis read an article about the sport, and she started to train her Collie, Pepper. Since then, Sandra has become one of the leading trainers in Freestyle, and has produced books and videos to help people get into the sport.

HEELWORK TO MUSIC VS FREESTYLE

At present, a number of countries have different interpretations as to the type of routine that is required

Skill and complexity have developed as the sport has taken off.

under the heading of Heelwork To Music. In the USA, Heelwork To Music is exactly what it says, i.e. heelwork performed with limited moves, set to a piece of music. There is also a category called Freestyle, which is a routine where anything goes. There is no requirement for the dog to be in the heelwork position, and the dog can work at any distance from the handler.

In the UK, in the early stages, there was just one category, which was Heelwork To Music, but there was no restriction on how little or how much heelwork was included. So some people started to produce what might be classed as a more Freestyle type of routine with very little heelwork. Some shows are now scheduling a Freestyle class, which will, hopefully, encourage handlers with breeds that are not natural heelwork exponents. In a Freestyle routine, the dog can be at any distance from the handler, and all types of moves are acceptable.

BREED CHOICE

This sport is available for any type of breed or crossbreed that is registered with the Kennel Club. Some breeds are known for being more difficult to train, but this is a test of the handler's skill and dedication, and the dog's individual character.

Inevitably, the Border Collie/Working Sheepdog tends to dominate, but other breeds are now being worked in competition. One of the first 'other breeds' to compete at advance level was Linda Topliss and her Rottweiler, Rory. This partnership has been an inspiration to many people, and now we have a diverse mix of breeds, ranging from a Bichon Frise to a Whippet – and even a Newfoundland – taking part in the same competition.

FITNESS

Regardless of the breed, it is very important that a dog is fit and healthy in order to complete some of the moves. As with Agility, some of the moves put strain on the joints (e.g. standing on the back legs), and should not be attempted until the dog is fully developed.

When you start working a complete routine, it is essential to start with a warm-up session. The dog may be asked to spin on the spot, walk backwards, and stand on his back legs – all of which involve parts of the body that are not in general use.

A human athlete will warm up gently before racing; so, with the dog, we may do some heelwork at various paces, or perhaps just give the dog a massage before starting training.

THE HANDLER

The beauty of this sport is that it is open to anyone, of any age. The routine is invented by the handler, so it can be adapted to suit the individual. It can be athletic or more sedate, depending on the handler's personal fitness, as well as working to the dog's individual strengths.

FINDING A CLUB

As the sport is growing, rapidly more and more classes are being set up. The best way to find a training club is to contact the various Heelwork To Music organisations, which should be able to give you names of members in your area. Contacting one of the journals that report on events can be helpful, as they may have lists of classes.

If there are no classes in your locality, you will need to read up as much as you can find on the subject. There are now a number of books and videos available. These are useful for those starting off in the sport, who want to know how to train the basics.

2 First Steps

Many people are now getting puppies specifically to train for Freestyle. If this is the case, you can start on some preliminary work to help with your dog's future career, as well as teaching the basic Obedience exercises.

Playing with your puppy is essential, as a dog that is play-motivated often has a happier outlook when it comes to work. In a Heelwork To Music context, the most important aspect to get the puppy used to is running through the handler's legs. It sounds straightforward, but it is an area where older dogs may have a hang-up.

Use your play session positively. For example, when the puppy is tugging on the toy, guide him round in a circle on the spot. This will get him used to a twist-type exercise without the pup being aware that he is being taught anything. The emphasis, however, is to take everything slowly and gently, planting the seeds for what you want the dog to do in the future.

REWARDS

There are basically two types of reward that can be used to motivate a dog: play and food. For Heelwork To Music, the challenge is to get the dog working without the hander having to hold the treat or the toy, but this is only required when the dog fully understands what is expected of him.

In addition to food and play, the handler has another powerful weapon in his armoury – the voice. It is very important that you use your voice to motivate the dog, as well as working with food treats and play. Communication between handler and dog is essential in order for the dog to understand that what he is doing is correct. In a competition, you can speak to the dog as much as you like, so it is an invaluable aid.

The more you play with your dog, the more he will become focused on his toy.

In my opinion, play produces a more enthusiastic working dog than one who is totally reliant on food. So, if your dog has a favourite toy, keep it just for training sessions, so that he has something to look forward to when you start work.

FOOD REWARD

Food can be useful to teach certain moves, but it must be used correctly in order to achieve the best results. Food rewards can be divided into categories A and B, and can be used depending on how confident the dog is with the move, and where he is performing.

Category A: These foods include liver, cheese and sausages, which are highly palatable to the dog. If you are in a new situation or you are teaching a new move, the dog will be more eager to perform it, as the reward is greater than normal. Don't get in the habit of always using the same reward, as this will become boring, and the dog will not put in as much effort as he can.

Category B: In essence, these are boring treats, such as wholemeal biscuits, which can be used at home where the dog is more confident and less distracted.

Some dogs respond better to food – but the treat should be worth working for!

> ## TRAINING TIP
> *If you have a small dog, attach the treat to a pole, or use a tube of cream cheese for when giving rewards. This will give you an extra few inches so that you will not have to bend down to get the dog to follow the reward.*

COMMANDS AND SIGNALS

It is up to each individual handler to decide on the commands or signals that are to be given to the dog. However, once you have chosen a command, you must stick to it. My advice is to use an obvious command for what the dog is doing, e.g. "Right" for when the dog is walking on the right-hand side in heelwork. When you have chosen the commands you will use, write them down so that anyone working the dog knows what commands to use.

At the beginner level you can give as many commands as you like, and you can talk to the dog throughout the routine. However, as the dog becomes more accomplished at moves, the handler can start to make the signals less obvious. This is an important step, as when you are performing at the higher levels, the signals or cues to the dog should be hidden in the body language of the handler.

TRAINING MOVES

When it comes to training the moves, it is very important that you apply a little-and-often method, rather than attempting a massive chunk of training in a day. You will find that Heelwork To Music training is much more mentally tiring for a dog than just doing basic heelwork.

TAKE YOUR TIME

When I am teaching a new move, I always try to help the dog as much as possible. This may mean putting the dog where I want him to be – either physically, or luring him with a treat. I only allow the dog to perform the move for two seconds to start with. It is much better to build moves up slowly, rather than going for the end move at the first stage. So, for example, when teaching the Go Back exercise (see page 40), I ask for only one or two paces backwards, and then I reward the dog so that he thinks it is really profitable to co-operate.

REWARD FREQUENTLY

It is important to reward frequently at the early training stage of a move. This will encourage the dog to look forward to doing as you ask, and he will be eager to carry on. At the end of every two-minute training session, I am looking for either a small improvement, or at least a quicker response than the last time that I taught the exercise.

BREAK DOWN THE EXERCISE

Some moves do take a long time to teach, and may need to be broken down into small stages. A good example of this is when the dog reverses around the handler. It is impossible to train this move all in one go; it needs to be broken down into smaller components.

SIMILAR MOVES

Some moves can appear very similar, so try not to confuse the dog by doing these exercises in the same session – unless the dog is confident in both. For example, if I was teaching Verse (see Chapter Four) in one session, I would not train Middle (see Chapter Five). The reason for this is that the dog may think that because he had just reversed back when he was in-between my legs, he should do that again and not stay in the Middle position.

AVOIDING ANTICIPATION

When a dog becomes confident in an exercise, it may mean that he will start to anticipate what you want. This can become a problem when you are working on a routine. If, for example, the dog starts to anticipate a twist, you must make sure you are not becoming too predictable in training. Start to mix and match. For instance, if the dog anticipates that, when you tell him to walk back, he is going to be asked to twist, then start varying it so you ask him to go back and bow, or to sit and beg.

DELAYING REWARDS

When the dog is confident in a move, it is important to get him used to the fact that he will be rewarded, even though you might not have a treat in your hand. The dog must understand that he needs to accomplish the move, and he will be rewarded by the owner taking the reward from his/her pocket, i.e. the reward is out of sight.

This is important for when the dog starts to compete, as no toy or treat can be taken into the ring. Work at this in early training so the dog realises that, although he cannot see the reward, it is still going to be worthwhile for him to do the moves.

> **TRAINING TIP**
> *When you are teaching your dog in the early stages, put some music on so that he gets used to the sound from the very beginning.*

WHERE TO TRAIN?

Most of the first training sessions should be done in a familiar place, such as at home, where there are few distractions. The beauty of Heelwork To Music training is that most of the moves can be taught in a very small area.

It is important to make sure that you train on suitable flooring. Many moves require the dog to have a good footing – carpet and grass are ideal. Some village halls are unsuitable for training, as they have shiny floors that can cause the dog to slip and injure himself.

CLICKER TRAINING

This type of training has become a very popular, fashionable method in teaching various moves in Heelwork To Music. However, as with any training aid, it has some weaknesses, which the handler should be aware of.

The clicker is only as good as the person operating it.

It takes no time for a dog to associate the sound of the clicker with getting a reward.

It can, therefore, be used incorrectly, so it is important to know how to use it effectively. The clicker is very useful for teaching technical moves, such as the dog putting his paw over his face. This is difficult to teach, as, if you say anything, such as "good dog", the dog will take his paw away from his face, and thus you are not rewarding the dog for the move you required.

I have trained all the moves outlined in the following pages by simply encouraging the dog with a treat to do what I ask. However, clicker training can be effective for some handlers, so here is a quick guide on how to use it.

Step 1: Firstly, the dog needs to associate the sound of the clicker with some type of reward. This is just a case of using the clicker and then feeding the dog a treat a few times, so that he knows that the click means a treat.

Step 2: Ask the dog to do something that you know he can do, such as "Sit". When he responds, click and treat. As soon as the dog realises that the click means he has done right and is going to get a reward, then you can start to use the clicker to train some moves.

Step 3: Even though the philosophy behind clicker training is that the dog works out what the handler wants, I always give the dog as much help as I can in order to get started. For example, if I want the dog to sit on a box, I will say nothing, but will stand by the box holding a treat above it. If the dog is interested in the treat, he may stand on the box with his front feet, so then I can click and treat. When the dog is confidently standing on the front of the box, I take the treat further back until he gets on the box completely – then I can click and treat.

The dog can be encouraged to place his paws on the box by holding a treat above it.

19

One of the problems that I have found with the clicker is that people tend to use it long after the dog has learned what is required. If I am using the clicker to teach a move, I get rid of it as soon as I can – usually within a day. When the dog understands what is required and is performing the move consistently, I quickly then use a command and get rid of the clicker.

Another problem that I have found, when taking clicker trained dogs in a class, is that they are not always reliable when it comes to producing a move that has been asked for. The dog may go through his whole repertoire of moves if the first one is not what the handler wanted, in a bid to earn his click. In the competition ring, the dog must do what you have asked for, rather than trying a move because he got a click for doing that in his last training session.

Obviously, you must choose the training method that works for you and your dog. If you decide to use clicker training, stick to the following guidelines:

- Use the clicker only when you are starting a move.
- Get rid of the clicker and put the move on command as soon as the dog is responding consistently.
- Help the dog as much as you can. You do not have to rely on verbal commands – you can use your body (particularly your hands and feet) to show the dog where you want him to go.

3 Basic Obedience Training

There are a number exercises that are used in Obedience competitions that can help when it comes to training and performing in Heelwork To Music. As has been mentioned earlier, the invention of Freestyle means that it is not essential to have a dog who performs perfect heelwork on the left-hand side. However, if the dog has some knowledge of the heelwork position, this will certainly help when teaching some of the moves.

Teaching your dog any Obedience exercise is important, as it will help your general control of him. The Obedience exercises outlined below are taught as for an English style of competition. If you are competing outside the UK, it would be advisable to look at the type of heelwork allowed in your country before you start training.

LEFT-HAND HEELWORK

This is the normal Obedience working position, and it can be taught in various ways. One of the best methods for teaching tight heelwork, on the left side, is by using a toy or a treat to reward the dog when he is in the correct position.

Step 1: To help the dog keep in position, hold the lead

1. To keep the dog in position, hold the lead close to your left leg.

2. Start with a few paces in a straight line.

close to your left leg with your left hand. Hold the toy or treat in your right hand, above the dog's head but close to your side, in order to keep the dog's attention.

Step 2: Start with a few paces in a straight line, giving the command "Close" or "Heel", and then progress to a small left-hand circle. Intersperse verbal praise with the "Close/Heel" command to remind the dog to maintain his position. It is important to remember to give the dog the toy/treat while he is close to your leg and looking up at you.

Step 3: After a period of time, the dog will realise that he is getting the reward for being on the left-hand side, close to the handler's leg. Then it is just a case of developing the amount of work, including changes of pace and changes of direction, which you can accomplish with the dog in position. For more help in this area, it would be advisable to find a local Obedience club to attend.

WATCH

It is imperative that you keep your dog's attention when you are in the ring, especially when there might be many hundreds of people watching you, as well as lots of things going on around you. Basically, the command "Watch" should mean that the dog looks up at your face – and nothing else – until you give the next command.

Step 1: This simple exercise starts with showing the dog a treat, and then positioning it underneath your chin. Talk to the dog, telling him how good he is, and inserting the command "Watch" now and again. To begin with, only ask the dog to "Watch" for a few seconds.

Hold a toy or treat under your chin to focus the dog's attention.

Step 2: Gradually build up the time period that the dog can pay attention to you. Then start to add distractions and practise in different areas, still asking for the dog's attention. This exercise will teach your dog to focus on you, regardless of where he is and what is happening around him.

INSTANT DOWN

This is a progression from teaching the basic Down position, and it can prove very useful if you can complete the move instantly in a Heelwork To Music routine. You can use it when you want the dog to stop on the spot, or it can be the start of a move (such as creeping along). All that is needed is to speed up the dog's response.

Apply a little pressure to the collar to encourage your dog to go into the Down.

Step 1: Run your hand down the lead to the collar, while commaning "Down". If you apply a little pressure on the collar, it will encourage the dog to lie down.

Step 2: When you have a good, fast response, progress with the exercise off-lead, increasing the distance between you and the dog.

RECALL

The Recall or Come in Front position, facing the handler, is very important in Heelwork To Music, especially if the dog is doing a Freestyle routine.

Step 1: Back away from your dog, holding the treat in front of you. The dog should come to the front, and then you can give the "Come" command and reward him.

Back away from your dog, holding a treat in front of you.

Step 2: Work on this so that, no matter where you move, the dog comes to the 'in front' position. Try doing a figure-of-eight, keeping the dog in front of you the whole time. This will help when you are developing routines.

Step 3: When the dog is confident in the front position, try to relax your hands so that it looks less like you are holding a treat in front of you, in order to get the dog to come.

WAIT

This command means that the dog should stop in whatever position he is in, and await your next command.

WAIT

1. Use your lead and a hand signal to reinforce the Sit position.

2. Step further back so your dog will "Wait" at a distance.

Step 1: Start by placing your dog in the Sit, with the lead above his head, so that you can use it to reinforce the Sit position. Tell your dog to "Wait", using a hand signal.

Step 2: Hold your hand up to form the Wait signal, and swivel from the heelwork position to the front of the dog. Praise him for staying in position.

Step 3: Go back to the dog's side and reward him in the Sit. Do not let him get up as soon as you return, as this can create problems later.

Step 4: Gradually back further away from the dog. Sometimes go back to the dog, and sometimes call the dog to you from the Wait. This is in order to avoid anticipation of the command to "Come".

Step 5: Introduce distractions to desensitise the dog to a variety of sights and sounds while he is sitting and waiting. This will help him to be secure while he is in position, which will help when it comes to performing in the ring.

RETRIEVE

It can enhance a routine if the dog is able to fetch an article, such as a hat. It does not have to be a formal retrieve, as in a competition, but the dog should be able to go and get the article the handler wants.

Step 1: Get two of your dog's favourite toys, and throw one of them a short distance. When your dog picks up the toy, encourage him to come back to you by using the other toy as an enticement. At this stage, it doesn't

RETRIEVE

1. Work on an enthusiastic retrieve.

2. Be ready with a second toy so you can do an exchange as your dog comes in.

matter if the dog drops the first toy; you are simply getting the dog used to returning with it.

Step 2: As you are throwing the toy, use the command "Fetch" or "Get it". If he drops the toy on his way back, encourage him to go and pick it up again and bring it closer, before rewarding him with the second toy.

Step 3: In time, you should be able to stand up straight, and the dog should bring the first toy in close, and sit in front of you.

Step 4: When the dog is retrieving consistently, introduce other articles for him to fetch.

POSITIONS ON THE MOVE

Although this is a more advanced exercise in Obedience competition, it is very useful in a Heelwork To Music routine. This is where the dog will go into the Sit, Stand, or Down position from the heelwork position, while on the move.

POSITIONS ON THE MOVE

1. Walk forward with your dog in the Heel position.

2. Give the command "Down" and continue to walk forward.

3. Swivel round, and praise your dog for staying in position.

Step 1: Make sure that the dog knows each position well before attempting this exercise. For the purpose of this section, I will outline the Down, as this is probably the easiest position to start with.

Step 2: Walk slowly forward with the dog in the left heel position. Command the dog "Down", and, as he drops, tell him "Down" again. Swivel from heelwork to the front of your dog, giving him lots of praise for staying in position. This similar to teaching the Wait command.

Step 3: Return to the left side of your dog, and reward him in the Down position.

Step 4: Gradually build up the exercise so that you can command "Down", and carry on walking forward without the dog for a short distance, and then return while he stays in position. Use the same method for teaching Sit and Stand on the move.

This exercise has many applications in a Heelwork To Music routine – for example, when the dog is being commanded to sit during heelwork. The handler walks forwards, then to the left, and then walks backwards down the opposite side of the dog until he/she is standing behind the dog, and gives the command to Verse. By teaching Sit on the move, this looks a lot smoother than stopping and then asking the dog to sit before carrying on with your routine.

4 Beginner Moves

It is important to remember that all dogs are individuals, and this can be seen very clearly when you are training moves for Heelwork To Music. You may find that your dog has a real liking for some moves, yet there may be others that he finds difficult and is reluctant to perform. My advice is: if a dog does not seem to like a move, do not force him. All dogs have their strengths and their weaknesses, and it is far better to concentrate on the positives. Try a move for a short while, and, if your dog does not seem comfortable with it (due to his build, his weight, his age, or because he is worried by it), leave that move out of his repertoire.

There are a number of moves that can be performed on the spot with the dog, and I have outlined these below. All of the moves are best accomplished with the dog off lead, but, if need be, use a lead rather than allowing the dog to go wrong.

TWIST AND WHIRLY

The twist is where the dog turns in an anti-clockwise circle on the spot in front of the handler, or from the heelwork position.

Step 1: Position your dog in front of you, and place a reward in your left hand.

TWIST

1. Hold a treat, and keep it level with the dog's head.

2. Use the treat as a lure so the dog moves in an anti-clockwise circle.

3. Reward your dog for completing a full circle.

4. Gradually, reward your dog after he has done multiple twists.

Step 2: Crouch down, and keep your hand level with the dog's head. Using the treat as a lure, take the dog around in an anti-clockwise circle, giving the command "Twist". When the dog completes the circle and is facing you again, give lots of praise and a reward. Remember to do only one twist, and then reward, so that the dog builds up a reward history in his mind.

Step 3: When the dog is doing the twist every time, gradually start to stand more upright. Continue giving some help, if it is needed, by dropping your hand back down to the dog's head level.

Step 4: Now start to ask the dog to do multiple twists before he receives a reward.

Step 5: Move a few paces backwards, and ask the dog to twist while he is coming towards you.

Step 6: When your dog can do a twist on the move, facing you, place him in the heelwork position and ask for the twist from there.

The 'whirly' is taught the same way, but place the treat in your right hand and guide the dog so that he turns in a clockwise circle. Use the command "Whirly".

TRAINING TIP

Only teach one direction at a time. Make sure your dog has mastered one direction before progressing to the next.

TWIST ON THE MOVE

1. The dog is commanded to "Twist" out from the handler.

2. Handler and dog Twist together.

USING THE MOVE

There are a number of options for using this move in a routine:

- Dog in the 'in front' position, the handler walks backwards, telling the dog to "Twist".
- Dog in the heelwork position, and is commanded to twist out from the handler and then back into the heelwork position. For extra effect, the handler and dog perform the same move simultaneously.
- When both directions have been taught, the dog is placed in the left heelwork position and is asked to "Twist". The handler turns in the same direction, but only does a half-twist, so that the dog ends up on the right-hand side of the handler. Then, the handler can ask for "Whirly", turning the same way as the dog, so that the dog ends up on the left-hand side again.

ROUND

As the command suggests, this is when the dog goes around the handler in a clockwise circle.

Step 1: Start with your dog in the left-hand position, with your legs together.
Step 2: Using your dog's training toy, bend down to your dog's level. Encourage him to follow the toy around, while you pass it from one hand to the other, in a clockwise circle. Use the command "Round".
Step 3: Gradually start to stand more upright, and command the dog to go "Round", but do not pass the toy from hand to hand.
Step 4: Ask the dog to go round multiple times before being rewarded.

> ### TRAINING TIP
> *If your dog begins to slow down when performing this move, go back to doing one round, then throw the toy forward as the dog comes into the left side. This should increase the dog's drive to go round quickly.*

USING THE MOVE

When the dog is able to circle the handler on his own, the move can be used in various other ways.

- Dog goes round handler, while handler moves in the opposite direction.
- Dog on the left side, the handler walks forward, tells the dog "Round", turns the opposite way, and then

ROUND

1. Use a treat to encourage your dog to go "Round" the back of your legs.

2. Reward the dog as he comes into the left side.

3. If you need to speed up the move, throw a toy as the dog comes into the left side.

4. This move looks effective if the handler turns the opposite way to the dog.

goes back into left-hand heelwork. The dog will be doing a half-round rather than a full one, circling the handler.

THRU

This is where the dog comes from any angle, races through the handler's legs, and then returns to the heelwork position.

Step 1: Position your dog, close up, facing you. Bend down to the dog's level, and place your left hand in the dog's collar.

Step 2: Open your legs wide, and then throw a treat through your legs. Let go of the dog's collar only when he is part-way through, and then tell him "Thru".

TRAINING TIP

It is essential to keep your hand in the dog's collar in early training and to guide him through your legs. It only takes one time of the dog going round your legs for him to learn this is a viable escape route.

Step 3: Start to stand more upright, and see if the dog will go through your legs without your hand in his collar.

Step 4: When your dog is confident running through your legs to follow the treat, he must learn to perform the move, even if he cannot see the treat being thrown. Start by holding your hands behind your back. Tell the

THRU

1. With a treat in your right hand, hold your dog's collar with your left hand.

2. Throw a treat through your legs, and guide the dog "Thru".

3. Reward your dog as he returns to your left side.

4. In time, your dog must learn to perform the move while you are walking away.

5. Reward the dog as he comes into the left-hand heelwork position.

6. Now you can link "Thru" with your next move.

dog "Thru", and then throw the treat. In this way, the dog is rewarded with a treat when he has completed the move, but he is not relying on the signal of seeing a treat being thrown.

> **TRAINING TIP**
> *Stand in a narrow hallway with your feet up against the wall so that the dog has no option but to go through your legs to get the treat.*

Step 5: When your dog is confident with the above step, it is time to start rewarding him in the left-hand heelwork position. This will give you a means of linking this move with another, at a later stage.

USING THE MOVE

• With the dog in the Sit, he is commanded to "Wait". The handler walks away and turns, telling the dog "Thru".

With smaller breeds, go down on one knee and command the dog to go "Thru".

39

- Dog on the left side, the handler walks forward, tells the dog "Thru", and the dog comes back into heelwork position. This gives the impression of the dog circling the handler's leg.
- With smaller dogs, the handler can go down on one knee and tell the dog "Thru".
- Dog in front, the handler walks backwards and commands "Thru", while continuing to walk back so that the dog comes to the front. This move looks better if it is repeated a few times in one space.

WALK BACK

This is where the dog is facing the handler, and the dog and handler (or just the dog) walk backwards.

Step 1: Position your dog in front of you in the Stand. The treat should be in your right hand.

Step 2: Walk towards the dog, pretending to throw the reward behind him, using the command "Back". First of all, the dog will only do one or two steps backwards – this should be rewarded.

Step 3: Gradually build up the distance so that the dog will go back with you.

Step 4: The next stage is to get the dog to walk backwards without the handler moving with him. Ask the dog to go "Back", and pretend to throw the treat behind the dog. When he has gone back a few paces, throw the treat behind him.

Step 5: When the dog is beginning to go back on his own, he may begin to stop after a few paces. This is

WALK BACK

1. Hold a treat in your right hand, and position the dog in the Stand.

2. Walk towards the dog, pretending to throw the treat behind him.

3. An alternative method with a large dog is to put the treat into his chest.

4. Gradually build up the distance the dog will walk back on his own.

TRAINING TIPS

- *If your dog bends to one side as he walks back, do the exercise alongside a wall so that he cannot bend that way.*
- *If you need to correct a bend, do not call the dog and walk backwards to get him straight in front. Stand still and encourage him to come into the front position. Guide him to come in straight by using your hands.*
- *Larger dogs sometimes have a problem with this move. An alternative method is to try holding a treat on the dog's chest, so that, when he looks down for the treat, he will take a few paces backwards.*

when you need to tell him "Back" again, and to try to get an extra pace back at each training session before you give a reward.

Step 6: In time, your dog should be able to walk back confidently at least six to eight foot (1.83-2.44m).

TRAINING TIP

Practise this move regularly, as your dog will stop making the effort to walk backward a long way if he thinks he can get the reward earlier.

USING THE MOVE

- Ask for a Walk Back of several paces, and then ask the dog to Twist.
- Start with the dog in the heelwork position, and send him "Back" so he ends up facing the handler's back.

VERSE

If your dog has learnt to walk back, then this move should follow on well. It can be used as a move on its own, or in conjunction with others. The basic aim is for the dog to reverse backwards through the handler's legs.

Step 1: Put your dog in the Stand, in the left-hand heelwork position.
Step 2: Place a treat in your left hand, and put your right hand in the dog's collar.
Step 3: Step across the dog's back, leading with your left foot, and use your right hand gently to push the dog backwards between your legs. Stand still, and give the command "Verse".
Step 4: When the dog has reversed all the way back, put your legs together, and reward the dog in the left-hand heel position. Again, it is important to think how you will link all the moves together – finishing in this position will enable you to continue with heelwork at a later stage.
Step 5: When the dog will reverse back confidently between your legs starting close up, work at increasing the distance that you stand behind him. Build the distance up gradually, otherwise the dog will turn around and come to you.

TRAINING TIP

If your dog is reversing back slowly, try to speed him up by allowing him to Verse, and then immediately throw his toy to him as he is coming into the heelwork position.

VERSE

1. Put your dog in the Stand in the left-hand heelwork position.

2. Hold a treat in your left hand, and hold the dog's collar with your right hand.

3. Step across the dog's back, leading with your left foot.

4. Place your right hand under the dog's chest.

VERSE

5. Use your hand to gently push the dog backwards through your legs.

6. When the dog has reversed all the way through, put your legs together, and praise in the left-hand heelwork position.

7. Gradually, stand further back from the dog, so he has to increase his reverse.

USING THE MOVE

- The handler stands behind the dog. As the dog starts to reverse, the handler turns around so that, as the dog Verses through, he ends up facing the handler.
- The dog is commanded to "Wait". The handler comes forward, then walks down the right side of the dog until he/she is standing behind him. This looks smarter than simply walking backwards from the left-hand heel position, with the dog in the Sit.

RIGHT

This is the command for the dog to be on the right-hand side in a heelwork position. The command to be on the left is taught in exactly the same way, with the dog working on your left (see page 21).

Step 1: Place your right hand in the dog's collar, and have a treat in your left hand.

Step 2: Hold the treat above the dog's head, but close to you, and step off in an anti-clockwise circle, using the command "Right". This will bring the dog in on to your leg.

Step 3: Once the dog holds the right heel position without being held by his collar, start increasing the amount of work the dog does on the right side. Try doing a figure-of-eight with the dog on the right; this will help him to use his back end.

Step 4: When your dog is confident on the right, you can combine this position with other moves that are performed on that side, e.g. whirly – see page 33.

RIGHT

1. Hold the collar in your right hand, and step off in an anti-clockwise circle.

2. When the dog is working close to your leg, you can release his collar.

CHANGE

Now that the dog has been taught to do heelwork on the left and right side of the handler, it is time to work out how to get him from one to the other. The main way of doing this (no matter what size the dog), is to do a half-twist. This is where the dog and handler move in the same direction as each other, so that the dog ends up on the right side.

The aim is for the dog to pass through your legs on to the right side, like the first part of a Weave (see Chapter

Five). However, you will need to put this on to another command so that the dog does not get confused about what you are asking him to do.

Step 1: With the dog on the left side, place a treat in your right hand, and bring your right foot forward.
Step 2: Show the dog the treat between your legs, tell him to "Change", and let him follow the treat through your legs to the right side. Command "Right", and take one or two paces forward, with the dog on the right. Then praise and reward.

CHANGE

1. Show the dog the treat between your legs, and tell him to "Change".

2. As the dog becomes proficient, you can stand upright, and move forward.

Step 3: When the dog performs the above step while you are standing still, try moving off in left heelwork. Slow down slightly as you place the right foot forward, and ask the dog to "Change". Drop your right hand down again, to attract the dog through. Then carry on for a few paces with the dog on the right, and reward.

Step 4: Gradually stand upright as the dog gains confidence. The move should become slicker, with the handler making a less obvious stop.

> **TRAINING TIP**
> *To get your dog to go back on to the left side, simply use the "Thru" command, as the dog should know that this command means 'go thru the legs and on to the left side'.*

ROLL

The Roll move is where the dog rolls over from left to right in front, or to the side of the handler.

Step 1: Start this move with your dog in the Down, preferably lying on one side.

Step 2: Use a treat, and encourage the dog to follow it so that he rolls over on to his other side.

Step 3: As the dog gets better at this exercise, the handler should stand up.

Step 4: When you reach the stage when the dog is very confident, the handler can start moving, and can command the dog to "Roll" either with the dog in front, or from the left-hand heelwork position.

ROLL

◀ 1. Use a treat, and encourage the dog to follow it.

▼ 2. The dog rolls over on to his back.

3. He is rewarded ▶ when he rolls back into the Down position.

Step 5: When the dog has accomplished a roll in one direction, he can be taught to roll back the other way. This should only be attempted when the dog is 100 per cent confident with his first roll.

BOW

1. Kneel next to your dog, with a treat in your right hand.

2. Lower the treat to the ground, at the same time tickling the dog's inside-back leg with your left hand.

3. Remove your hand from the dog's back leg, and increase the time he stays in position.

BOW OR BEND

The Bend command is frequently used instead of Bow, which can be confused with the Down command. This move is often used to begin or end a routine.

Step 1: Kneel on the floor next to your dog, and have a treat in your right hand.

Step 2: Hold the treat at the dog's nose, and lower it to the floor. At the same time, use your left hand to tickle the dog on the inside of the back leg. Hopefully, he will end up with his front end in a down but the back end standing up. Tell the dog to "Bend", and reward him while he is in position.

Step 3: Gradually remove your hand from the dog's back leg, and increase the time he holds the position by telling him to "Bend" and then "Wait".

TRAINING TIP

When rewarding your dog, throw the treat into his chest, between his legs. When you start to stand up, the dog will be less reliant on your hand being on the floor, as he anticipates that the treat will be thrown into this area.

5 Action Moves

This is a more advanced part of training, as both handler and dog must move together. As with all moves, do not start work on this stage of training until your dog can perform the moves confidently on the spot.

LEFT-HAND HEELWORK

As mentioned in the basic Obedience section (Chapter Three), you will find that a dog who can hold a nice left-hand heelwork position will be a bonus during a routine. Apart from moving forward with the dog, there are two other directions that can be used: dog and handler walking backwards, and dog and handler walking sideways.

WALKING BACKWARDS

Step 1: Put your dog in the left heelwork position, in the Stand.
Step 2: Keep your dog's attention, give the command "Close", and take one or two paces back. Encourage the dog to stay by your leg, and reward.

Keep your dog's attention, as you step back a few paces.

Step 3: Gradually build up the number of paces that the dog can walk back in the heel position.

WALKING SIDEWAYS

Step 1: This is easier for the dog than walking backwards. Firstly, treat this as a static exercise. Tell your dog to "Wait", take a step to your right, and run your left hand down the dog's lead, saying "Close" and manoeuvring him into the left heelwork position.

Step 2: When your dog can do this one step, tell him "Close", and move together to the right for one pace. Then reward.

Move together to the right for one pace, and then reward.

Step 3: Now the dog should be able to build up a few paces moving to the right.

TRAINING TIPS

- *If you have a dog who finds it difficult to walk backwards in a straight line, position him against a wall. This will keep him straight and in position.*

- *To make this move look tidy, remember to cross your left foot over your right foot.*

WEAVE

1. Encourage the dog to follow a toy as you pass it from one hand to the other.

2. The dog should pass through your legs and emerge on the right side.

3. He comes back through your legs to the left side.

WEAVE

This has become one of the most common action moves. It is where the dog weaves through the handler's legs while they are both moving forward.

Step 1: Stand on the spot, with your legs apart, holding a toy/treat (in both hands if using food), with the dog in the left-hand heelwork position.

Step 2: Tell the dog to "Weave" as you pass the toy from one hand to the other in a flowing manner. The dog will pass from the left, through the legs to the right side, then through the legs back to the left side. When he has done a figure-of-eight around your legs, reward.

Step 3: Build this up slowly until you can stand up straight and tell the dog to "Weave" on his own.

Step 4: When the dog is able to do this – and only then – you can start to walk forwards. At first, walk just a few paces and then reward the dog.

> ### TRAINING TIP
> *As the dog becomes more confident, it is important that the handler extends his legs in order to present a tidy picture.*

USING THE MOVE

- The Weave can then be used on the spot or when moving.
- The handler can walk backwards while telling the dog to "Weave".
- When the dog is confidently doing the Weave, you can teach him a more flowing backwards weave called Fly (see Chapter Seven).

MIDDLE

During a routine, it is important that the team moves around the ring. Training the dog to move in-between the handler's legs allows this to happen in a different manner to heelwork.

Step 1: To start this move, simply get the dog in-between your legs, holding a treat out in front of you at arm's length.

MIDDLE

1. Position the dog between your legs, and hold a treat in front of you.

2. Move forward a few paces, and reward your dog in the Middle position.

3. When the dog is confident, you can start walking back together, with the dog maintaining the Middle position.

Step 2: Move forwards a few paces, reward the dog, and tell him "Middle", while he is in-between your legs.
Step 3: When the dog is comfortable in this position, and is moving forwards well, start moving backwards together, telling the dog "Middle". No matter which way you go, the dog should stay in the middle.

USING THE MOVE

- With the dog in the Middle position, go forwards and then circle the dog around one leg. Start by teaching this standing still, letting the dog follow the reward around one leg, and then back to the middle.

USING THE MOVE

1. Start with the dog in the Middle position.

2. Circle the dog round one leg, and back to the Middle position.

- Use another command, and teach the dog to hold the same Middle position, this time with the dog facing the opposite way to the handler.

OVER

As the command suggests, this is where the dog will jump over some part of the handler, or jump over a prop that is used in the routine. It is important that the dog is fully developed before he starts any jumping work. If the dog is trained in Agility, this move will come very easily.

Step 1: To teach the dog to jump, start by holding a pole against the wall. Ask the dog to jump, using a command such as "Over". Keep the pole very low, and reward a successful jump.

Step 2: Gradually increase the height of the pole. When the dog is jumping confidently and understands the command, you can work on jumping different hurdles.
Step 3: When your dog is happy with the above step, he can start to jump over your leg, or over your whole body. The same command can be used to get the dog to jump through a circle made with the handler's arms.

OVER

1. Position a pole against a wall, and encourage your dog to jump, using the command "Over".

2. Gradually increase the height of the pole.

3. Progress to teaching the dog to jump over your leg.

SIDE

1. Position the dog in front of you. Hold a pole in your right hand and a treat in your left hand.

2. Move the pole to the side of the dog, so that he steps away from it.

3. When your dog is confident, you can get rid of the stick, and he will still move to the side.

SIDE

This crab-like move requires the dog and handler to step to the side while facing each other.

Step 1: Place your dog in the front position, facing you. Hold a treat in your left hand, and a pole in your right hand. The pole is simply there to act as a 'moveable wall'.

Step 2: Place your left hand in the centre of your body, then move the pole towards the side of the dog. He should start to move away from it (i.e. to the handler's left), so tell him "Side", and reward him after one pace.

Step 3: Build up the number of paces that the dog can achieve walking sideways. Make sure he stays straight in front of you – if his hindquarters start to bend, the move looks untidy.

Step 4: Now the dog can crab to the side nicely, it is time slowly to withdraw the use of the pole. If the dog is confident, he will hardly notice when it is taken away.

Step 5: Using the same method, you can teach the dog to go back the opposite way. I use the command "Dance" for this move.

TRAINING TIP

When a dog is very confident with the move, he may start to get over-excited and over-turn his body in the direction that you are going. If this happens, the pole needs to be brought into the opposite side, i.e. holding it in your left hand to stop the dog bending in that direction.

6 Crowd-pleaser moves

Heelwork To Music is performed in front of an audience, so, when planning a routine, it is important to include some moves that have special appeal.

WOGGLE

This is actually a combination of three of the basic moves that you have already been taught, namely: Verse, Twist and Back. Remember to use a command that is different and that can be instantly recognised by the dog. So, by dropping the W off Woggle we use the word "Oggle", as it is something completely different to any other command.

Step 1: To teach this flashy exercise, your dog must have a strong Verse move (see page 43).
Step 2: Put your dog in the front position. Place your right hand, palm outwards, in the dog's collar on the left side as you look at him. Hold a treat in your left hand, and keep this hand by your side.
Step 3: Turn your right hand anti-clockwise until the dog is facing away, but straight in front of you, ready to Verse. Give the command to "Oggle".
Step 4: Then, tell the dog to Verse backward through your legs. As soon as he has completed the move, put

WOGGLE

1. Place your right hand, palm outwards, in the dog's collar.

2. Turn your right hand anti-clockwise, so that the dog is facing away from you.

3. The dog can now Verse back through your legs.

4. The dog comes back to the left-hand heelwork position.

your legs together, and reward the dog on the left-side heelwork position

Step 5: In time, the dog will not need your hand in his collar, and, when you tell him to "Oggle", he will turn and reverse.

Step 6: Up until now, this move has been executed directly in front of the handler. To progress the move, try sending the dog back a few paces and then asking for "Oggle", so that the dog backs through your legs. This move looks particularly flashy if it is performed when the dog is at a distance from the handler.

Step 7: When your dog is doing this move confidently, you need to be able to link it to other moves. You can do this by telling the dog to "Oggle", and then turning around so that the dog reverses through your legs and ends up facing you. This will enable you to tell the dog to go back and "Oggle" again, as he has ended up facing you and is not in the heelwork position.

UP ON BACK

This move always gets the crowd going when you are performing a routine. The dog places his paws on the handler's back, and then the pair move forwards. Again, it is important that this move is not performed with a young dog.

Step 1: To start this move, use a toy to present a target for the dog to get hold of.

Step 2: With the toy in your hand, kneel down and place your right hand over your right shoulder.

UP ON BACK

1. With the dog behind you, use the toy as a target. Kneel down slightly so the dog gets the toy.

2. Gradually stand up straighter.

3. Start to drop your hand down in front of you to make it look more natural.

Step 3: Position the dog behind you, and then ask him to walk forwards and get the toy, using the command "Up". At this early stage, it may be easier to get a friend to hold the dog and to point out to him where the toy is.

Step 4: As the dog becomes more familiar with where the toy is located, the handler can start to stand more upright. Remember to reward the dog when he goes up on the back, and do not keep him in position for too long.

Step 5: As the dog builds up the muscles in his back legs, he will be able to remain in position for longer. You can encourage this by holding the toy up out of the dog's reach, but always drop the toy down to the dog when you reward him.

Step 6: When the dog is confident about getting 'up on back', the handler can move forward a few paces with the dog remaining in position. Remember to reward frequently to give the dog confidence.

Step 7: Gradually drop your right hand down in front of you, so that the dog stays up, even though he cannot see the toy. Reward your dog by dropping the toy over your shoulder – in this way you will both look more natural as you move forward.

Another method of teaching this move is to encourage the dog to jump up for a treat when he is facing you. As he does, tell the dog "Up" and reward him. When you ask the dog to put his paws on to your back, he will have some idea as to what is required of him.

HIGH

This move suits the smaller or more agile dog, as it requires him to stand on his own back legs. The previous exercise will help the dog to build up muscles in his back legs to support his weight, but if your dog is of a heavier build, it may be advisable to leave out this move.

Step 1: Position the dog in front, and hold the treat in your right hand. Now hold the treat above the dog's nose. As he takes his front paws off the ground to get the treat, tell him "High". Reward with the treat.

Step 2: To begin with, the dog will only stay in position for a few seconds. Gradually build up the time he stays on his back legs by holding the treat out of his reach.

HIGH

1. Hold a treat above the dog's nose to encourage him to go up on his back legs.

2. Progress the move by getting the dog to walk forwards.

3. In time, he will be able to turn a small circle.

TRAINING TIP

Build up the time your dog stays in seconds rather than minutes. If the dog is rewarded regularly, he should progress well.

Step 3: When your dog can maintain the position for ten seconds, try to get him to move backwards or forwards. The direction will depend on the dog – some find it easier to go in one direction than the other.

Step 4: When the dog is in the High, you can progress the move by allowing him to follow a treat around in a small circle above his head, thus doing a pirouette on his back legs. This is easier for smaller dogs, who tend to be more balanced. For more ways to vary this move, see Chapter Seven.

CREEP

A dog that performs this move well often gets the "ahhhh!" factor from the audience. As the command suggests, the Creep is where the dog crawls along the floor, on his belly. If you have a larger breed, it may not be easy for him to creep, so, as a compromise, the dog could creep with his front end down but keep his back end up, as in a bow (see page 51).

CREEP

1. Kneel by your dog, and allow him to follow a treat along the ground, in the Down position.

2. As the dog understands what is required, you can begin to stand more upright.

Step 1: To teach the Creep, get down on the floor with the dog in the Down position.

Step 2: Allow the dog to follow the treat in your hand, across the floor, a short distance. It is important to use your "Down" command interspersed with the "Creep" command to start with, as the dog will probably try to get up out of the Down position.

Step 3: As the dog builds up confidence in this position, and stops trying to get up, you can start to stand more upright, still keeping your hand low to the ground.

Step 4: When your dog can perform the Creep over a distance of 6 ft (1.83m), it is time to withdraw the hand signal, and rely on using the verbal command. The best way to achieve this is to kneel on the floor with your legs apart, and with your hands behind your back. Ask the dog to "Creep" towards you, and, as he reaches you, drop the treat behind your legs so the dog can see it in-between them. As you are kneeling, the dog only has a small space to go through, and so, hopefully, he will remain in a Creep position. This will teach him that he is being rewarded for being on the floor in a Creep, rather than for getting up.

TRAINING TIP

Do not give the treat straight into the dog's mouth, as this tends to encourage him to reach up out of position. Always give the treat down into the dog's chest, so he has to look down for the treat.

USING THE MOVE

- The dog Creeps while in the left-hand heel position.
- The dog is left a distance away and told to "Creep" back to the handler.
- The Creep is combined with a roll every few feet.

WIGGLE

This is where the dog performs a circle, backing around the handler. It is a fairly difficult move to teach, but, when the dog masters the Wiggle, it can be stunning to watch.

There are various ways to teach this move. I developed a method that, if the handler gets it right, works for dogs of all sizes. It is very important that the handler knows what he is doing, so it is advisable to work out where your hands and legs go in relation to the dog, before you actually start training with him. Prior to teaching the dog to back around both legs, concentrate on getting the dog to reverse around your left leg first.

Step 1: Start by sitting your dog on the left-hand side. Hold the treat in your right hand, and place that hand on your right knee.
Step 2: Place your left hand in the dog's collar, and take your right foot back over the dog's back.
Step 3: Tell the dog "Wiggle". Alternatively, tell him "Back", as it sometimes is easier to start with a familiar command and then introduce the command "Wiggle" when the dog is doing the first part of the move well.

As the dog reverses through your legs, let go of the collar. He will just be reversing straight back and then taking the treat from the right knee.

Step 4: Do not step quite as much across the dog's back, and then you can use your right leg as a buffer to get the dog to reverse in more of a circle around your left leg.

Step 5: To start with, the dog will be doing a U-shape from the left-hand heelwork position to the front, facing you. The reason for holding the treat on the right knee is as follows. When your dog can Wiggle from the left-hand heelwork position to the front position, his body will be in the correct place to continue reversing back into heelwork position if he is used to taking a treat from the right knee.

At this stage, it does help if the dog knows where his heelwork position is on the left side. If the dog is struggling, the handler can bring the treat back over the dog's head, guiding him to walk backwards into the heelwork position.

TRAINING TIP

Don't go for the complete Wiggle at once – it is essential that this move is built up in stages. With larger breeds especially, it helps if you keep your left hand in the collar and hold the dog's head away from your leg. This has the effect of making the back end move around more.

WIGGLE

1. Position the dog on the left side, and hold a treat to your right knee.

2. Place your left hand in the dog's collar, and take your right leg over the dog's back.

3. Tell the dog "Wiggle", and encourage him to reverse through your legs.

4. As he comes out of the reverse, he takes the treat from the right knee.

WIGGLE

5. After achieving the half wiggle in front, then encourage the dog back to the heel position.

6 & 7. When your dog can circle your left leg, close your legs, and ask for "Wiggle" so that he circles both legs.

Step 6: When your dog can complete a full Wiggle around the left leg, it is very easy to get him to circle both legs. Tell the dog to "Wiggle" but keep your legs tight together so the dog should reverse around them both.

USING THE MOVE

- When your dog is confident doing the Wiggle, the handler walks forward and gets the dog to Wiggle during some heelwork.
- The handler turns in the opposite direction to the way the dog is backing, making the move look even more spectacular.

GIVING PAWS

Asking your dog to put his paws up on command may seem a very simple thing to do, but it often gets a positive reaction from the crowd. The important point to remember is that it works better in a routine if the dog puts his paws up high. This has big appeal, especially with the larger breeds.

The commands I use are "Foot" and "Feet", but any combination is okay, as long as the dog knows which paw to raise. Some handlers use the same command for both paws, but I think this is confusing for the dog if you are asking for a specific paw.

Step 1: Start with the dog siting in front of you, and place the treat in your right hand.
Step 2: Pick up the dog's left foot with your left hand,

GIVING PAWS

1. Pick up the dog's foot, and tell him "Foot".

2. Hold your hand so that it is just out of reach. This will encourage the dog to raise his foot higher.

3. Gradually stand more upright, and reduce hand signals.

4. You can progress this move by teaching the dog to kick out his legs in front of him.

and, as you are looking at him, tell him "Foot" and give him a treat.

Step 3: As the dog gets used to your hand picking up his foot, he should start raising the foot by himself. At this point, the dog must learn that by hitting his paw on your hand, he gets the reward.

Step 4: To get the dog to raise his foot higher, hold your hand up so it is out of the dog's reach. The dog will make an effort to touch your hand; he may not reach it, but he can be rewarded for bringing his foot up high.

TRAINING TIP

It is important to give the treat from the hand that the dog is not touching. The dog may not perform the move in competition if he is used to getting a treat from the hand he touches, and then finds it empty.

Step 5: When you are getting a good, consistent response with one paw, it is time to start work on the other paw. This is trained in exactly the same way, but using a different command, e.g. "Feet".

Step 6: When each paw is being given on command, put the dog into the heelwork position, and ask him to give his paws from this position. This will allow you both to kick your legs forward at the same time.

TRAINING TIP

When working with the dog giving his paws from the heelwork position, it is easier to ask him to touch your left hand with his left foot.

Step 7: Gradually, the handler should be able to stand up straighter and reduce hand signals, but the dog should still kick his paws out the front of him. To progress this further, move forward while asking the dog to kick his feet forward. You may need to start the dog in a Stand for this.

BEG

As the command suggests, this is when the dog sits in a Beg position with his front feet off the ground. Small dogs find this move easier, but it can be more striking if the dog is bigger. In all cases, be careful with older dogs, as this position puts strain on the dog's back.

Step 1: Place the dog in front of you in a Sit position.

TRAINING TIP
When training this move, position the dog up against a wall to give him extra balance.

Step 2: Ask the dog to give a paw. Hold the treat above his head, and, as he reaches up for the treat, the other foot should come off the ground. When the dog is in the correct position, give the command "Beg", and reward.

Step 3: With practice, the dog should be able to maintain the position for a longer period, still using the support you are giving by holding his paw.

Step 4: At this stage, it is time to start to withdraw the hand that is holding the paw. To begin with, allow your

BEG

1. Ask your dog to give a paw, and hold a treat above his head.

2. As the dog reaches up, the other paw will come off the ground. Command "Beg" and reward him in this position.

3. To begin with, allow your dog to stay in position for just one second before rewarding.

4. In time, your dog will be able to maintain the Beg for longer periods.

dog to stay unsupported in the Beg position for just one second before rewarding.

Step 5: As the dog gets more accustomed to getting his balance, he will be able to hold the position for longer. You must now stand more upright and try holding the treat out of the dog's reach.

Step 6: Again, it is just a case of progressing the Beg until the dog can hold it for longer. You can then try walking around the dog while he is in the Beg position. This is when a good Wait command comes in useful (see page 26).

7 Advanced Training and Moves

There are many ways that you can advance your dog's training simply by using the basic moves outlined so far. There are three main areas to proceed with advance training, which are as follows.

HANDLER POSITION

It is easy to forget that the handler can change the look of a move by simply changing position. However, as the handler is changing his stance, this needs to be taught so the dog still understands what is required.

Start by listing your dog's strongest moves, then think of the positions you could be in when you ask the dog

The dog performs a High facing the handler's back.

The same move, but this time the handler is kneeling down, facing the dog.

to complete the move. For example, if the dog is in the High move, on his back legs, you have the following options:

1. Handler standing facing the dog.
2. Dog facing the handler's back.
3. Handler kneeling down with the dog in the High.
4. Handler turning around while the dog is in the High.

DISTANCE TRAINING

This follows on from the last point, getting the dog to perform various moves but at a distance from the handler. To begin with, it may mean that you have to teach the dog to walk back further on his own or to do a good Wait while you walk away. When you have worked on this, you can train the dog to perform other moves at a distance, such as:

1. Dog doing a Twist.
2. Dog in a Bend.
3. Dog doing Paws Up.
4. Dog doing Roll Over.
5. Dog in a High at a distance.
6. Dog in a Down and then doing a Creep back to the handler.

To start training moves at a distance from the handler, the dog must be very confident in the move that you are asking for. I use two methods for getting a dog to work at a distance:

You can work on your distance training by placing the dog behind a barrier.

Method 1: Place the dog behind a small barrier, which prevents him from moving forwards. Gradually, ask the dog to perform the move as you move backwards away from the dog.

Method 2: Place the dog on a mat on a linoleum kitchen floor. The dog will probably prefer to stay on the mat, so he will not come forwards. Then, proceed as above.

TRAINING TIP

When you reward your dog for doing something at a distance, make sure he does not come forwards for the reward. It is better to throw the toy behind the dog when he has done the move. If he comes forward while doing the move, send him back until he reaches the place where he started the move, and reward him there. The dog must realise that it is more profitable to do the move at a distance than up close to the handler.

ADVANCED LINKING

As your dog develops more moves, you can link certain moves together that are more difficult. For example, get the dog to jump your body, then go underneath you and jump again.

Alternatively, you could ask the dog to Creep and Weave at the same time. There are many options in this section; just use your imagination and see what you can come up with.

Here are a few suggestions for you to try.

1. Send the dog back a distance, then do the Side move.
2. The dog faces the handler and jumps the right leg out to the Side, then turns into the Middle and circles the right leg.
3. The dog in heelwork position, kicks each leg out, then does a Wiggle around the handler as he gets back to the heelwork side. Both walk back with the dog in heelwork.
4. The dog faces the handler's back. Both walk backwards, then the dog is asked to "Whirly" behind the handler.

FORWARD

This is where the dog will walk forward of the handler, and then reverse down the right-hand side of him, ending up back in the left-hand heelwork.

This move works well in line dancing/Western-theme routines, as it looks as if the handler is doing a do-si-do with the dog.

FORWARD

1. Hold a treat at arm's length in front of you, and encourage the dog to take it.

2. After treating the dog, command him to "Verse" back through your legs.

Step 1: Before attempting this move, it is essential that the dog can perform a good Verse; if not, go back and review this move.

Step 2: Hold a treat in your right hand, allow the dog to follow the treat forward of you, telling the dog "Forward".

Step 3: Reward the dog when he is at arm's length in front of you. Practise this a few times before going on to the next stage.

Step 4: Bring the dog forward. When he reaches your hand, ask him to "Verse" back through your legs. By now, the dog should have started to realise that when you bring your right hand forward, he is to go forward of you.

Step 5: When the dog can Verse back after coming forwards well, it is just a case of putting your legs together to get him to reverse down the right side of you. Reward the dog in the left-hand heelwork position.

> **TRAINING TIP**
> *Sometimes the dog does not keep his body straight when reversing down the right side, so make sure you have a wall on your right when you are training, so the dog has to reverse straight in-between your leg and the wall.*

Step 6: Gradually build it up so that you can do three forwards before rewarding the dog, as this move looks better if done in batches.

> **TRAINING TIP**
> *Go back on a regular basis and reward the dog for coming an arm's distance forward of you. It is easy for the dog to start taking a short-cut and not walking forward far enough.*
>
> *Spend more time practising the dog coming forward and reversing between your legs, as this will keep him straighter when it comes to reversing down your right side.*

HEAD

This is a useful position, as it enables the handler to move around the ring without having the dog in heelwork. For this move, the dog should keep his head on the side of the handler's right leg, facing the opposite way to the handler.

HEAD

1. From the front position, encourage the dog to follow the treat until your right hand is on your right side, and the dog's head is level with your leg.

2. When the dog can remain in position, start to walk backwards. You can then progress to doing a clockwise circle.

Remember to work out how you are going to get the dog into this position during a routine. From the start, get the dog into the habit of going round, then into this move. These two moves will flow together, as they are both in the same direction.

Step 1: Hold a treat in your right hand, and place the dog in front of you.

Step 2: Encourage the dog to follow the treat until your right hand is on your right side, and the dog's head is level with your leg. Tell the dog "Head" and reward.

Step 3: Repeat the above step, and gently press the dog's head on to your leg so that he associates this place with the command and reward.

Step 4: When the dog can gain the position with the handler standing still, start to walk backwards with the dog in that position, keeping your hand on your side. When the dog can do a few steps in this position, do an anti-clockwise circle, as the dog will find this direction easier to start with.

Step 5: When the dog can stay in this position while you move around in a circle, start to walk forwards, as this will mean the dog has to walk backwards. Only do one or two paces, as the dog is very likely to come out of position. Gradually build the time that the dog is in the position until you can move forwards and backwards with the dog.

> **TRAINING TIP**
> *If your dog is toy-motivated, try putting the toy under your right arm and then rewarding the dog by dropping the toy down to him.*

USING THE MOVE
To progress this move, you can teach the same position on the left side, then change the dog from one side to the other by asking him to "Twist" or to "Whirly" in front of you.

FLY
This move is best taught when the dog is doing a good, basic Weave. Basically, this is a backward weave that flows better than doing an ordinary figure-of-eight

FLY

I. Position the dog in front, and take a step forward with the right foot.

2. Use the treat to encourage the dog to go behind your right leg.

3. Step back a pace, and encourage the dog back to your right side.

weave backwards (see page 55). The dog needs to take a slightly different line into the Weave. Note that the dog will be facing the opposite way to the handler, who is going to be walking backwards.

Step 1: Position the dog in front, and hold a treat in each hand. The dog is going to enter the Fly by going behind your right leg, and then around your left leg.

Step 2: Take a slight step forward with the right foot, and encourage the dog around behind the right leg, then through to the left side. Then step back with that right foot and encourage the dog back to the right side, telling him "Fly", and rewarding.

Step 3: Repeat the above step several times, then add another step backwards. Gradually build up the number of steps, and try to stand more upright, holding your hands out to the side rather than down with the dog.

SIDE BEHIND

Earlier, the dog was taught to walk sideways to the handler's left when he was in front of the handler. Side Behind is basically getting the dog to do the same move, but facing the handler's back.

Step 1: Position the dog facing you in the Stand. Tell him to "Wait", and turn your back to the dog, holding a toy in both hands behind your back.

SIDE BEHIND

Holding a toy, turn your back on the dog and tell him to "Wait".

Take two paces to the right, give the command "Side", and then reward the dog.

Step 2: Remembering that, to the dog, Side means facing the handler and moving to the left, Side Behind means the dog is facing the handler's back, and the handler needs to step to the right. Start by taking two steps, telling the dog "Side", and then rewarding.

Step 3: Build up the number of paces to the side before rewarding the dog.

> **TRAINING TIP**
> *Work out how you are going to get the dog into the Side Behind position during a routine, and practise it as a separate move. For example, tell the dog to "Verse", then get him to "Stop" and "Side Behind".*

OUT

This move is easier with Collie types, as they naturally circle the handler, but any dog can be taught to do this with a little help. It requires the dog to go out away from the handler and to do a big circle around. The move looks better if the dog is at least 6 ft (1.83m) away from the handler.

The method I use to start this move depends on the dog's temperament.

METHOD I

I use this for the toy-motivated dog, who is eager to follow a toy when it is in the handler's hand.

Step 1: Start by holding the toy at arm's length. Dogs seem to have a natural preference for going clockwise or anti-clockwise, so find out what your dog is most comfortable with. Encourage the dog to follow the toy while you turn around in a circle on the spot. Work at getting the dog to stay as far from you as possible.

Step 2: When the dog is just a little further away than normal, reward him by throwing the toy over his head, so he has to run away from you to get it. Hopefully, the dog should remain further from you, anticipating that the reward will be thrown over his head. Now start telling the dog "Out" when he is circling you.

METHOD II

If the dog does not naturally walk out from you when you turn in a circle, or is not interested in toys, try the following method.

Step 1: Use a small, bendy fence to make a big circle. Stand inside the fence, with the dog on the outside.

Step 2: Stand close to the fence, and encourage the dog to go around, telling him "Out" and motivating him with your voice. When you reward the dog, throw the treat over his head (see Method I).

Step 3: Gradually position yourself further from the fence, in the middle of the circle. If the dog is anticipating the treat being thrown over his head, he should stay further away from you. When he is running around the circle of the fence, occasionally throw the treat a little further around the circle to encourage the dog to move round.

Step 4: In time, the dog will learn to move on his own, while the handler circles in the same direction.

OUT

1 & 2. Encourage the dog to follow the toy by holding it at arm's length, and turning a circle on the spot.

3. In time, the dog will be able to work at a greater distance from the handler.

Step 5: At this stage, take the fence away on a random basis. However, do not do too much without the fence, as the dog will come in closer to you.

USING THE MOVE

When the dog is capable of running around the fence until you stop turning, there are two ways to further progress this move.

- The handler can stand still while the dog runs around the handler at a distance.
- The handler moves around in the opposite direction to the dog.

Both of these options are easy to teach if the dog has had good basic training in the move, and has not been moved on too quickly.

TRAIN

This move is more difficult for the dog, as he will need to have his back to the handler. In the Train position, the dog should be straight in front of the handler, but facing the same direction, hence the command "Train" (i.e. like a train on a track!).

If you have been teaching the Forward move (see above), the dog might attempt to do this move when you start the Train exercise. It is therefore important not to practise both moves in the same session until the dog is confident in both.

Step 1: Position your dog on the left-hand side, showing him a treat or toy in your left hand. Bring both hands together, and take them in front of you at arm's length. Encourage the dog to follow your hands

forward, tell him "Train", and reward after a few seconds.

Step 2: Repeat as above, but this time tell the dog to "Wait" when he comes forward of you. Give the command "Train", praise and reward.

Step 3: Now the dog should see your outstretched hands as the signal that he is to go into the Train position in front of you. Tell him to "Wait" when he is straight in front of you. Then stand up straight,

The signal for the Train position is both hands held in front of you.

keeping the dog in position, and reward.

Step 4: As soon as the dog is happy to go into the Train position, you can start to move in one direction. The dog will find it easier to move forward, so encourage him to follow the treat a couple of steps forward, before getting the reward.

USING THE MOVE

When the dog can move in the Train position, the options are down to the individual handler and dog. My suggestion is to tell the dog "Side" when he is in the Train position, so that you both move to the right, facing the same way.

USING PROPS

When you are performing, you can use a prop, such as a walking stick/cane or a hat, that will go with your costume. The prop can be used in the routine to create different moves.

WALKING STICK

JUMPING THE STICK

If your dog has been taught the command "Over", this move can be used in conjunction with a stick in the following ways.

If the dog has learnt the command "Over", this can be used for jumping over a stick.

- The handler holds one end of the stick. The dog goes round the handler, then jumps the stick as the handler turns in the opposite direction.
- The handler holds the stick at both ends, and positions it in front of the dog. The dog goes through the handler's legs, and then jumps the stick (which is held at the handler's left side), as he comes into the left-hand heelwork position.

GOING ROUND THE STICK

This is where the dog circles the stick while the handler either remains still, or walks around the stick in the opposite direction to the dog. The dog should have already been taught to circle the handler, so we can use this familiar command to start the dog in the move.

Step 1: Place the stick in your left hand, and rest the end of the stick on the floor in front of you. Hold a toy in your right hand, and position the dog at heel.

Step 2: Use the toy to encourage the dog to set off in a clockwise direction around the stick. It sometimes helps to move your left foot up to the base of the stick to start

GOING AROUND THE STICK

1. Position the dog on the left-hand side, and rest the stick on the ground just in front of you.

2. Place your right foot at the base, then use the toy to encourage the dog to set off in a clockwise direction.

3. Work at keeping the dog close to the stick, giving the command "Go round".

4. Take the dog in a complete circle round the stick before rewarding.

5. In time, the dog will be able to "Go round" the stick while the handler is also circling.

the dog off in the correct direction.

Step 3: Encourage the dog to follow the toy around the stick fairly close, giving the command "Go Round". Allow the dog to circle once, then give the toy as a reward.

Step 4: Gradually increase the number of times the dog will circle the stick. At the same time, move your hand to the top of the stick, and start to decrease the use of the toy as a lure.

Step 5: At this stage, the dog should be able to go forward and circle the stick, while the handler holds both hands (plus the toy) on top of the stick. When the dog has circled a few times, drop the toy down as a reward.

Step 6: Now hold the toy in your left hand, which will be on the top of the stick. Tell the dog to "Go Round", and start to move in an anti-clockwise direction around the stick. Allow the dog to circle once, then drop the toy.

Step 7: The dog should be able to circle the stick, with the handler standing still or moving anti-clockwise. Using this method, you can now teach the dog to circle the pole in the opposite direction, perhaps starting the dog from the right side.

WEAVE WITH THE STICK

The dog is required to weave through the handler's legs, around the stick, and then back through the handler's legs. It is similar to the weave in Agility, although in this instance, the dog must do a continuous weave one way, then go back the other way. The command that I use for this move is "Extra".

Step 1: Place the dog in the left-hand heelwork position. Hold the stick in your left hand, and rest the end on the floor, out to your left side.

Step 2: Holding a treat in your right hand, encourage the dog to start a figure-of-eight around your legs. This is the same as when you taught the Weave (see Chapter Five). As the dog gets back to the left side, let him follow the treat around the stick in an anti-clockwise direction, and then reward him as he comes by your left side.

Step 3: Continue doing this until the dog, on the command "Extra", weaves around the legs and then around the stick. Encourage the dog to continue weaving so that he completes the move twice. Then reward your dog.

Step 4: When the dog is confident with where he is going, start to tone down the hand signal to get the dog to go around the stick. This will mean you can stand upright.

Step 5: When the anti-clockwise direction is mastered, you can use the same method to teach the dog to do this move, but with the stick in your right hand.

If you are particularly quick, you can combine both moves by switching the stick from one hand to the other as the dog is weaving through.

Remember to give generous praise when the move is completed.

WEAVE WITH STICK

1. Hold a toy in your right hand, and encourage the dog to come through your legs.

2. The dog circles your right leg, and comes back through your legs.

3. As he comes out on the left side, take him to the stick.

4. Encourage the dog to circle the stick.

5. He has now completed the move.

FEET OVER STICK

By holding the stick between your hands, the dog can jump up and put his paws over it. The handler can then move in any direction.

Step 1: The dog should already know the command "Up" (see page 64). Command "Up", and hold the stick at either end, in front of you.
Step 2: Place a toy under your chin, and ask the dog to get "Up". Let him place his paws over the stick, tell him "Up", and drop the toy from under your chin.

Place a toy under your chin, and hold the stick at either end. Use the command "Up" for this move.

Step 3: Gradually build up the length of time the dog stays in position with his paws on the stick.
Step 4: When the dog is confidently jumping up and putting his paws on the stick, you can then start to move. Start by taking a few steps in one direction and then reward the dog. Build up the distance that the dog will stay up on the stick when moving.
Step 5: Now take the toy away, and start to reward the dog after doing the move. Remember, without the toy, you will need to use lots of verbal praise to encourage your dog to stay in position.

FIGURE-OF-EIGHT/AWAY

This is where the dog does a figure-of-eight around the handler and an object, such as a hat or a stick. The command is "Away".

FIGURE OF EIGHT

1. Start by circling the dog around you.

2. When he returns to your left side, approach the box.

3. Then, use a toy to encourage the dog to go round the box in an anti-clockwise direction.

4. When the dog goes round to heel, he has completed a figure-of-eight.

Step 1: Find a large object, such a box, at least 18 ins square (45 cms), and position the dog in front of you.

Step 2: Place a treat in your right hand, and then tell the dog to go round you. As the dog comes into the left-hand side, encourage him to follow the treat around the box in an anti-clockwise direction, telling him "Away". When the dog comes back to the front of you, he will have completed a figure-of-eight.

Step 3: In time, the dog should know where he is going, so he will not need to follow a treat. Now reward the dog when he has gone around the box, around you, and back into the left-hand heelwork position. This will allow you to go on to another move.

> **TRAINING TIP**
> *Place the box in a corner of a room, so that the dog has a pathway around the box to follow.*

Step 4: Build up the number of times that the dog does the figure-of-eight, and also the distance that you stand from the box.

USING THE MOVE

During a routine, you can use the hat or stick, instead of the box. Do not practise too much on a small object, as this move looks better when the dog take a wide berth around the object.

8 Music, Maestro!

W hen your dog is able to do a variety of moves, you are ready to find a piece of music for your routine. It is often helpful to choose music that the audience and the judges will recognise, as this will enhance their enjoyment.

Do not choose a piece of music just because you have always liked it, or because it is by your favourite artist. When performing Heelwork To Music, there are a variety of factors that need to be taken into consideration, such as the speed of the music in relation to the movement of the dog.

MUSIC TYPES

There are definitely some pieces of music that are easier to work with than others. Listed below are the four main types that are useful for a Heelwork To Music routine.

Foot on beat: This type of music has a walking beat, so that when each – or just one – foot hits the ground, it is on the beat of the music. An example of this is *We Are Family* by Sister Sledge. This is probably the best type of music to go for when preparing for a first performance.
Count the beats: This is where you need to count the beats. For example, count to four constantly, i.e. 1,2,3,4

twist 1,2,3,4.

Split sections: If the music has no lyrics, you may need to break the music down into sections and time each one, so that you have an idea of how long each piece of the track is.

Lyrics: Tracks that have lyrics can also make a performance easier, as you can have 'marker words' which signal when to perform a specific turn or move.

ROUTINE THEME

The theme of the routine should also be taken into consideration when choosing music. The theme may take various forms – for example, an Irish dancing theme or a track from a movie. I have used the *Great Escape* soundtrack, and reflected moves in this, such as crawling along the floor with the dog on my back.

The Great Escape: This move was designed specifically to fit the music.

Some tracks will have no clear theme, and these can
be easier to construct routines to. The music is fairly
general, and moves can be performed in a variety of
places. It is not essential to have a theme, but it can help
to tie the dog and handler together, especially if the
handler has a good costume.

COSTUME

If you are using a theme, then your costume should
follow it. For example, in the *Great Escape*, I dress as a
prisoner. The costume should not detract from the dog,
and it is essential to ensure that nothing is hanging
down that is going to distract him when he is working.
If you are doing moves with the dog going through
your legs, the dog should have a clear run through.

It is not always necessary to have a costume, it is just
as important that you provide a clean and tidy image
(i.e. no trainers or sportswear), as you may lose marks
for being an untidy handler. One advantage with having
a costume is that you can hide behind it – it can give
you the confidence to perform to the best of your
ability.

BREED OF DOG

Your dog's breed or general appearance can give you
inspiration for choosing a piece of music. For example, a
flashy Poodle suits a more extrovert track, or an
American Cocker Spaniel might do a American line-
dancing routine. It is also important that the speed of
that track suits the pace of both dog and handler.

EDITING THE MUSIC

Having found a piece of music with the potential for a
Heelwork To Music routine, the next area to examine is
the length of the track. To start with, you need to find
out what length of time you will be expected to perform
in a competition. This will depend on the organisation
that is running the competition, so find out what is
required, as points may be deducted if you over-run.

When you have found out the time allocated for your
routine, you may need to edit your track. In order to
decide what pieces of music you want from the track,
listen to it and note down the time, in seconds, of the
pieces that you would like to be put together.

When you have made your selection, you can contact
a local DJ to edit the track, or you can purchase a piece
of software for your computer that can do the same
thing.

When you have your track, make a few copies of it on
to tape. Keep the original just for performances so that
it does not get worn out. Then, in practice, you can
rewind or forward the tape to your heart's content. The
next stage is to listen to the track hundreds of times so
that you know every word, and every twist and turn of
the music. It is important that you are really aware of
the music before you start putting moves to it.

HANDLER AND MUSIC

Some people have natural rhythm when it comes to
working or moving with the music, but not all of us are
that fortunate! So it is important to look at improving

The routine should look polished, with dog and handler working in harmony.

your own movement to music before you put the dog into the equation as well.

How do you do this? Well, it is not essential that you move with the music, but some gestures or movements by the handler will help the routine look polished. One way to improve your rhythm is to join a dance local class. Regardless of whether you are doing line-dancing or ballroom dancing, it should give you some idea of how to move to music. Alternatively, you could go and dance your heart out at a night club, but, if that is not to your taste, make use of family occasions when the music comes on, and get up and dance. This will also give you confidence when you come to perform with your dog, in front of people.

9 Putting A Routine Together

Before starting to construct a routine, it is important to be aware of what the judges will be looking for. There are three main areas they will assess:

Programme content: The judges will be looking for a programme with varied content. Repetition of moves can be valid (e.g. heelwork), but continual repetition should be avoided, as this could result in a lower mark. I try to use a particular move only twice in a routine, but I may use a move in batches, e.g. three Thrus, one after the other.

It is important to make full use of the ring during the performance; marks may be deducted for the team staying only to the boundaries of the arena.

The judges will also be evaluating the dog and handler as a team, watching how they interact, and assessing whether the moves complement each other. However, the emphasis should be on what the dog is doing.

The judges can also mark down teams in this section if they are not tidily dressed, so it is important to have a clean and tidy image when you enter the ring.

Note: Contact the organisation that you are going to compete under, as some will have rules as to which types of moves you can do in certain classes.

Accuracy and execution of movements: The judges will be looking to see how well the moves are executed, and how accurate they are. If something goes wrong, try to disguise the mistake by going on smoothly to the next move. This section will also take into account the bearing and deportment of the handler, which should be smart and not cramped. In addition, the judges will be assessing the dog's style, which should be happy and willing.

Interpretation of moves: Although the judges will be looking for some reflection of the music in the routine, it is not necessary for the handler to move in time to the music. However, some musical interpretation is needed to score well in this section. The gestures of the handler will be taken into consideration, but should not play more of a part in the routine than the dog's moves.

LINKING MOVES

When you have got your music to the right length and know it back to front, then you need to start linking moves. This involves combining some of the moves that you have been doing separately. For example, Heel, Twist, handler and dog turn to the right, then Whirly the dog to the left heel side. In this way, you are combining left and right working, and also Twists and Whirlies.

When you come to putting the moves to music, you will find that some will flow together, while others appear to stop and start. I always try to get my moves to

LINKING MOVES

For this Mission Impossible routine, the dog has learnt a series of linked moves, which tell a story and fit the music.

flow forwards. For example, do not go from a Weave to a Walk Back – this would entail stopping violently and trying to turn the dog around quickly to get him to Walk Back. It would be better to go from the Weave into heelwork forwards, or you can get away with calling the dog out of the Weave and walking backwards yourself.

The next step is to list all the moves that the dog, and you *and* the dog can do together. Also list which moves you feel your dog links together well in training, e.g. Heel Twist, Heel Twist. Don't forget that moves can be executed from all sides, i.e. facing, left, right and behind.

When you have listed the moves that you can link together, try to visualise performing them to the music. Remember that you need to move around the ring, so make sure that some of the linked moves enable you to move to other parts of the ring during the performance. It is also important to mark which of these moves your dog performs best. This may be simply because the dog does a move well, or it may be a difficult move that not many dogs can achieve.

IDEAS FOR LINKING BASIC MOVES
- Dog in right heelwork position, and commanded to "Roll". The handler jumps the dog into left heelwork.
- Back, Back, Twist, Come, Come, Twist.
- Dog in a High. The handler walks back, tells the dog "Thru", and then "Weave".
- Dog in Wait. The handler walks behind, tells the dog to "Verse", then, as he gets through the legs, tell him

"Up on back".
- Dog in front. The handler walks back, and commands: "Go thru, Go thru, Come", then "Twist, Twist, Roll" in front position.
- Round, Thru, Round, Thru.
- "Wiggle" one leg, "Wiggle" two legs.
- Dog in Middle. The handler commands "Down" and "Roll".

CHOREOGRAPHING A ROUTINE

When you are putting a routine to music, it is advisable to attend a show and watch the advance classes to see how they achieve an effortless transition from one move to another. You can also see how the music is used to interpret moves with the dog. If you cannot get to an event, you may be able to get hold of a video of a show. This will give you an idea of what works together, what looks good, and what a top-class performance looks like.

START AND FINISH

Before working on the whole piece of music, it is important to decide on your Start position. An innovative Start position is very important, as it will make the judges and audience sit up and take notice. As many people start their routine with the dog in the heelwork position, you will need to think about the look of your Start, as you will be static for a while until the music starts. I use a Start which is different – but relevant to the music – in my *Great Escape* routine. I start on all fours, with the dog underneath me in a

The Start position for the
Great Escape routine.

A classic Finish for this Western
routine.

Down, then we both Creep forwards together.

You also need to work out how you are going to move out of the Start position, as you will need to flow forwards or backwards to continue with the routine.

There are two options for the Finish:

Finish on a pose: Finishing with a static pose can be difficult, as it requires good timing and precision to end on the correct piece of music. If you are running late in the routine, it can then throw the end, which will look out of place.

Finish on a move: This method of finishing is easier, as you can put the dog into a move that he will be able to maintain until the music ends. For example, the dog can be in a High, or Up on back. This means that if you are late or early getting to the end of the routine, it does not matter.

CREATING A ROUTINE

Now that you have a list of your dog's moves, and you
know the piece of music that you are using very well, it
is time to think about putting the moves to the music. It
is not essential that your dog performs all his moves in a
routine. It is sometimes better to do a few good moves,
with everything flowing, rather than attempting a mass
of unrelated moves, one after the other. Here are a few
steps to creating a routine to music.

Step 1: Write out the lyrics of the song or break the
song down into sections and note the length (in
seconds) it runs for. Then write down your Start
position.

Step 2: Listen to the music, and visualise where certain
moves can be placed. Mark these against the words or
instrumental section on your sheet. Remember to
underline the key lyric word which will be your signal
for a specific move or change of direction.

Step 3: Go back to the start of the music. Take the first
15 seconds, and keep playing it until you can visualise
what moves you can do. When you start listening to
music for a routine, you should find that the music
speaks to you and tells you, for instance, where to
position a Weave. Remember that you need to move
around the ring. You might have the dog in the front
position and do a wiggly pattern, rather then staying in
a straight line, keeping the dog in this position until you
get to a bit where you can see a move.

Step 4: Gradually build the routine, taking each section

PUTTING IT TOGETHER

*When you have fitted the moves with the music, the
routine should flow, and appear effortless...*

at a time and marking the key words. Before you carry on to the next section, make sure that you are not repeating a move too frequently, and that there is sufficient movement around the ring.

Step 5: When you have put it all down on paper, it is time to walk through your jottings. When you start to walk through the routine, make sure you are in an area that is similar in size to the competition ring.

> **TOP TIP**
> *Remember that a move is not cast in stone – they can all be shifted around when you start putting the routine together.*

Step 6: After doing a number of walk throughs, you will find that bits need changing. It may be that the link you thought would flow, does not work out in practice, or you may think that another move would fit the music better. When you do have a final version of your routine, it is essential to walk it through until you know exactly where and when you should be at every point. If you are still working this out when the dog is with you, he will quickly become bored and switch off.

Step 7: When you are happy with the routine, it is time to work out a route plan. This is similar to planning a round in an Obedience competition. Start by placing an X in the middle of a sheet of paper. Then draw lines in different colours, marking moves on the sheet. This will enable you to see how you are using the ring.

TOP TIP

Remember where the judges are sitting, and try not to have your back to them, especially if you are doing a static move.

Step 8: Break the routine into sections, and then, with or without the music, work the dog in the correct order of moves. Working the dog into the equation can often change the routine. For example, you may have planned for four twists, but the dog can only do two.

Step 9: When you are at this stage, the routine should be roughly complete. Once in a while, do the whole routine, but don't do it too often as the dog could get bored or start to anticipate moves. It is better to practise a section at a time.

Step 10: It will be hugely beneficial if you can get someone to video your routine at this stage so that you can see how it all goes together – it can be very revealing!

Step 11: Now it is just a case of getting the dog used to the specific links of moves that you are using, and you should also be able to walk through the routine without really thinking about it. This is important as, when the nerves kick in as you enter the ring, you will be so familiar with the routine that you can just go on autopilot!

A SAMPLE ROUTINE

Here is a lyric sheet for the first minute of the track *We Are Family*, by Sister Sledge. The moves flow from one to another and there is a mixture of movement and static moves. The commands are highlighted so you can see what the dog would be told.

WE ARE FAMILY

The instrumental starts with the handler on one knee and the dog in an **up** with his feet on the handler's chest. From there, the dog goes **round** and **over** the knee, **round** again then under the knee and **round**, then **over** the knee, and **round** again.

The handler gets up and puts the dog into the **head** position, moves off with the dog in a clockwise semi-circle, sends the dog **round** forward into heelwork, then **thru** three times on the spot, while the handler moves the opposite way, ending up with the dog in the front position, facing the handler while the handler walks back.

WE ARE FAMILY	From **come** on "WE", tell the dog **back, back** then **twist** on the end of "FAMILY".
I'VE GOT ALL MY SISTERS WITH ME	**Come, come** then **twist** on "ME".
WE ARE FAMILY	Repeat as before: **back, back, twist.**

GET UP EVERYBODY AND SING	Repeat above, then **come twist** on "SING". Then the handler turns around at the same time as the dog **twists**, so the dog comes out of the twist and puts his paws **up** on the handler's back.
WE ARE FAMILY	Paws on back until the end of "FAMILY", then the handler turns so that the dog is in an **up**, but with his paws on the handler's chest; the handler walks into the dog.
I'VE GOT ALL MY SISTERS WITH ME	Handler turns on "ME", so that the dog's paws are on the handler's back again.
WE ARE FAMILY	Repeat, as before.
GET UP EVERYBODY AND SING	Repeat, as before, then do a right turn so that the dog has to drop off the front of you into left **heelwork**.

EVERYONE CAN SEE US TOGETHER	Few paces of heelwork.
AS WE WALK ON BY	**Weave**, then, on "BY", the dog goes into left **heelwork**.
AND WE FLY LIKE BIRDS OF A FEATHER	On "FLY" tell the dog to go **round**, while you turn the opposite way.
THOUGH I WON'T TELL NO LIE	On "LIE" the dog is told to go into **middle** as he gets behind the handler.
ALL THE PEOPLE AROUND US SAY	Dog in the **middle**, walk forward at "SAY".
CAN THEY BE THAT CLOSE?	Then **circle** the dog around one leg and walk backwards with the dog in **middle**.
JUST LET ME STATE FOR THE RECORD WE'RE GIVING LOVE IN A VILLADROME	On "RECORD" **circle** the dog around the leg again and walk forward until "VILLADROME". Then tell thedog to go **round** from the middle into left **heelwork**.

WE ARE FAMILY	Dog in heelwork. On "FAMILY" both stop. Dog puts his **paw** up, and the handler kicks his leg forward at the same time. Then walk back with dog in heelwork position.
I'VE GOT ALL MY SISTERS WITH ME	Then left about-turn from walking backwards on "ME", so you will be walking in the opposite direction than last time.
WE ARE FAMILY	Walk forward with the **paw** and leg up again on "FAMILY", as before.
GET UP EVERYBODY AND SING	Then walk backwards with the dog in heelwork.

USING A ROUTINE

I am often asked how many times a routine should be used. Normally I will only use a routine for three competitions, making small changes each time just to make it different for everybody. A lot of time and effort goes into putting a routine together, so it is impossible to put a new one together for every show. It usually takes one show for me to decide if I like the way that it has worked – no matter how many times I have done it in training.

> **TOP TIP**
>
> *Always be on the look out for your next piece of music. Don't be afraid to use a piece that someone else has used, as your performance will be completely different.*

PUBLIC DEBUT

Now that you have the routine fixed in your mind, and you have been working on it with the dog, it is time to get ready for a public performance.

Ease your way into competition with a few low-key events.

- One of the first things to do is to take the dog to different places to train the routine, making sure you use a place that is similar in size to the competition ring. This is where a portable CD player comes in handy. Moving training areas will accustom your dog to working in different environments.
- Another factor that can affect the dog is the audience clapping at the start of the routine. To overcome this, use tapes of people clapping at different levels, which will help to desensitise the dog.
- When you are confident that the dog can work the routine, you need to get used to performing in front of an audience. Ask friends and family to come and watch you train, as this will place you under more pressure. It is often more nerve-racking working in front of a few people than when you are faced with a big audience at a competition.
- You are now ready to take your performance into other situations. The best way forward is to contact organisers of local events and ask if they would like a performance, or you could see if the local home for the elderly would like a demonstration. The advantage of doing this is that you will get used to coping when the dog goes wrong, and you will learn to carry on as if nothing has happened. It will also give you confidence, as members of the public are often hugely impressed by the dog doing the most basic of moves.

10 The Competition

S tart by contacting the organisation that is holding the event, and ask them to send you a schedule. With the increase in the amount of classes available, it can sometimes be confusing as to whether your dog's routine fits the Freestyle or Heelwork To Music category. If you are unsure of which class to enter, ask the show secretary or an experienced competitor. Don't forget to send your payment with your form, otherwise it will not be accepted.

DAY BEFORE THE SHOW

By this time that the nerves should have really set in, and you will be wondering why you ever thought that competing was a good idea! However, if you have done the training, you and the dog should be fine.

THINGS TO PACK

- Make sure your costume is in good order, together with any props that are required for the routine. There are usually places to change at the venue, so don't wear any part of the outfit until the performance, as you never know what may happen during the day.
- Make sure you have at least two copies of the music that you are using. Mark it with your name, the dog's name, and the class that you are entering. It is

essential that you have two copies, as it is not unknown for tapes to get eaten in the recorder or for CDs to get scratched.

- Take rewards for the dog, especially if the dog has a favourite toy, as this can be used when you are warming up.
- Don't forget to take food and water for the dog, plus food for yourself.

DAY OF THE SHOW

This is what all the training has been for, so make sure that you arrive at the venue early, especially if you are in the first class. Start by booking your music in with the organisers, as you don't want to be running around like a headless chicken two minutes before your performance!

At most events, the organisers will let the competitors practise in the ring before the start or during breaks. So get the dog in the ring, and let him have a look around – there may be pots of flowers or speakers at ground level, which could distract the dog if he has not seen them before the performance.

Now start to get the dog's attention, and do a few moves that he likes, as this will give you both confidence.

If there are any parts of the routine that you are worried about, practise the links, but remember to help the dog. At this stage, it is better that the dog gets it right with a lot of help, rather than doing it wrong and you both becoming stressed.

TOP TIP

Do not over-do the practice. The purpose is not to work through the whole routine, but to familiarise the dog with the ring and to him working.

Find the time to watch the competitors before you, so that you have an idea as to what happens. When your performance time approaches, take your dog outside and make sure he relieves himself – you may also need a trip to the WC! Do not hang around outside the ring for too long before your turn, as your nerves will transmit to your dog.

The day of the competition when, hopefully, all your hard work will pay off.

IN THE RING

When it comes to your turn, remember to take a big, deep breath and *smile*! This is so important, as it makes you look as though you are here to enjoy yourself – even though you may feel petrified! Usually, the compere will introduce you and your dog to the audience, and then you must walk confidently to the middle of the ring.

If you have opted to take the dog in on the lead, you will need to remove it and give it to the steward. I always take my dog in off-lead so that we can go straight into a move, such as a Bow. If you don't want to do this, just acknowledge the judges, and then get the dog into the Start position, making sure you are facing the judges. When you are ready, nod to the sound man, and off you go…

When you come out of the ring, there will be a short wait while each judge scores you for each of the sections. This score is averaged and the final score will be announced.

SUMMARY

Your first competition will probably not be as bad as you feared. Once you start to analyse each section, you will realise that the dog did do the majority of what you asked for. Remember that a routine will never be completely perfect.

Before you leave the show, make sure that you have a copy of your marks, as this will give you some indication of how you can improve next time. Go home and think about the routine, reflecting on how each bit

Practice makes perfect – but remember, there is always another day – and another competition.

felt. If you are lucky enough to have a video of the performance, watch it, and decide what bits you liked and what bits you would rather leave out.

It is always important to remember how far you have come with your training. Be happy with what you have achieved, and how much progress you have made. Above all, make sure your dog knows that you think the world of him, regardless of how highly you have scored in competition.